BUDDHISM FC

- Learn The Way Of The Buddha -
- Take Your First Steps On The Noble Path -

By Luna Sidana

Table Of Contents

INTRODUCTION 2

CHAPTER 1: WHAT IS BUDDHISM? 5
SIDDHARTHA GAUTAMA & THE ORIGIN OF BUDDHISM 6
THE NATURE OF A "BUDDHA" 11
BUDDHISM TODAY 12

CHAPTER 2: THE WORDS OF THE BUDDHA 13
WHAT ARE THE SUTRAS? 17
DHARMA & "THE FOUR RELIANCES" 20
THE KALAMA SUTTA, OR KALAMA DISCOURSE 25
WHAT IS THE ABHIDHARMA? 29

CHAPTER 3: DIFFERENT TRADITIONS 32
THERAVADA 34
MAHAYANA 42
VAJRAYANA 44

CHAPTER 4: THE THREE MARKS OF EXISTENCE & THE FOUR NOBLE TRUTHS 49

CHAPTER 5: BUDDHIST COSMOLOGY 58

CHAPTER 6: THE FIVE SKANDHAS 63

CHAPTER 7: THE THREE POISONS & THE THREE JEWELS . 69
THE THREE POISONS 69
THE THREE JEWELS 74

CHAPTER 8: THE FIVE PRECEPTS & THE EIGHTFOLD PATH 78

CHAPTER 9: MEDITATION 89
CLASSIC MINDFULNESS MEDITATION — STEP-BY-STEP 93
MANTRAS 96

CHAPTER 10: BUDDHISM IN EVERYDAY LIFE 100
PRACTICAL APPLICATION OF BUDDHISM 102
SPREADING PEACE & LOVING-KINDNESS 103
SERIOUS HARDSHIP & ADVERSITY 107
PERSPECTIVE ON LIFE, MILESTONES & RELATIONSHIPS 110

CONCLUSION 116

© Copyright 2018 by Pine Peak Publishing - All rights reserved

In no way is it legal to reproduce, duplicate, or transmit any part of this document in either electronic means or in printed format. Recording of this publication is strictly prohibited and any storage of this document is not allowed unless with written permission from the publisher. All rights reserved.

The information provided herein is stated to be truthful and consistent, in that any liability, in terms of inattention or otherwise, by any usage or abuse of any policies, processes, or directions contained within is the solitary and utter responsibility of the recipient reader. Under no circumstances will any legal responsibility or blame be held against the publisher for any reparation, damages, or monetary loss due to the information herein, either directly or indirectly.

This document is geared towards providing exact and reliable information in regards to the topic and issue covered. The publication is sold with the idea that the publisher is not required to render accounting, officially permitted, or otherwise, qualified services. If advice is necessary, legal or professional, a practiced individual in the profession should be ordered.

Respective authors own all copyrights not held by the publisher. The information herein is offered for informational purposes solely, and is universal as so. The presentation of the information is without contract or any type of guarantee assurance.

The trademarks that are used are without any consent, and the publication of the trademark is without permission or backing by the trademark owner. All trademarks and brands within this book are for clarifying purposes only and are the owned by the owners themselves, not affiliated with this document.

Introduction

Buddhism is one of the world's oldest spiritual traditions — having existed for more than 2500 years. It's currently practiced by more than 480 million people all across the globe.

While countless religions have been abandoned through the centuries, the insights and practices of Buddhism are still carried on today in every corner of the world.

This is most likely because they resonate so strongly with the fundamental characteristics of our lives as human beings, and line up surprisingly well with much of our current scientific understandings.

While the core teachings remain the same, many aspects of Buddhist belief and practice have evolved differently in three major traditions across the Asia-Pacific region.

Buddhist beliefs and practices are motivated by the desire for relief from suffering. These practices offer a path to truth and enlightenment, centered on the realization that attachment and impermanence are the origins of suffering.

In this beginner's guide, we will provide the basic outlines of the understanding of the world that informs Buddhist practice.

Key concepts and terms will be introduced one by one. In this way, it will be easier to grasp the way Buddhists see the world and the nature of human existence. This is vital to learn if you aim to walk the path yourself.

Understanding key concepts – enlightenment, true self, the nature of reality, and the causes of suffering – are fundamental to guiding meditation practice and a Buddhist way of life.

Once we have introduced the core Buddhist teachings and provided an introduction to the traditions, we will explore the Eightfold Path to enlightenment, and the nature of essential Buddhist practices such as meditation.

You will learn about the nature of existence, the cosmos, reality and the place of conscious life within this grand, infinite arrangement.

Be prepared to venture onto a road of great discovery and inner peace.

Chapter 1: What Is Buddhism?

"Having gone on his almsround, the sage should then go to the forest, standing or taking a seat at the foot of a tree.

The enlightened one, intent on jhana, should find delight in the forest, should practice jhana at the foot of a tree, attaining his own satisfaction."

- Buddha

What we know today as Buddhism originated with one man and his quest to understand, and gain relief from, suffering.

The story of his life and pursuit of truth serves as a model for all the followers of Buddhism today.

Both what he saw to be the truth and how he lived are central to the tradition.

Siddhartha Gautama & the Origin of Buddhism

Scholars believe that the founder of Buddhism was Siddartha Gautama, also known as Sakyamuni, meaning "the sage of the Shake tribe."

Siddartha Gautama was an upper-class prince in an area that is part of modern day Nepal. It is believed that he lived between 563 and 483 B.C.E.

Although he was born into wealth and privilege, he spent most of his life seeking truth and the release from suffering.

In his early life, Gautama was shielded from the ills of

the world by his father, who hoped his son would seek prosperity and power within their social sphere.

According to Buddhist texts, Siddartha Gautama experienced four visions that eventually led him on his path of seeking truth:

1. First, he saw on old man, helpless and weak.

2. Second, he saw a man afflicted with a debilitating disease.

3. Third, he saw a mourning family group carrying the dead body of a loved one to its cremation. Age, sickness and death clearly caused suffering for human beings.

4. Siddartha Gautama's fourth vision was of a calm and serene man who lived as a recluse.

    This vision gave him hope that relief from suffering was possible.

Initially, Siddartha sought truth and peace in the opposite of his life of comfort. He decided to live as a wandering ascetic (as did many people during this time in Indian history and culture), and practiced self-deprivation in many forms.

During this time, when Siddartha was approximately 35 years old, he sat down under a Bo tree to meditate. The legend of the Buddha tells us that he meditated there for 49 days.

He is said to have been tempted by demons, and yet he continued to sit and pursue truth and peace through the meditative state.

According to legend, Siddartha became a Buddha, an enlightened one, after meditating deeply under a full moon, at the break of day, as the morning star appeared.

He had finally found the key to relief from suffering, the four truths of existence, that he had been seeking all this time.

Buddha thanked the Bo tree for sheltering him during his many days of meditation, and took his leave. From that time on, it was known as the Tree of

Enlightenment (the Bodhi tree).
Siddartha Gautama – the Buddha – had discovered a "middle way" between self-denial and sensual pleasures and luxury. His middle way consists of following what is known as the Eightfold Path, and coming to fully know the Four Noble Truths of existence.

Through his meditation and enlightenment, Siddhartha was able to see things as they truly were. He had seen that the cause of suffering is greed, selfishness and ignorance.

He saw that if people could rid themselves of these negative influences, they could find peace. Once he had achieved enlightenment, his followers came to call him "the Buddha", or "enlightened one."

The Buddha himself chose to be a teacher and mentor to others, and lived the rest of his mortal life as a wandering, mendicant sage.

He taught that there are Four Noble Truths about existence.

These truths are as follows:

1. Existence is suffering

2. Attachment and desire are the root of suffering.

3. It is possible to achieve release from suffering (Nirvana).

4. There is an Eightfold Path which can lead one from suffering to Nirvana.

This path has eight aspects, because it encompasses the way we think, talk, interpret the world, what we do, the actions we choose and the way we see the world.

Only when all these aspects of ourselves reflect and embody the noble truths, can we finally be released from suffering.

Buddha reached enlightenment on his own, by focusing his energy on seeking truth. He teaches that each of us is capable of doing the same – with

extensive practice and by training our entire selves, body, mind, emotions, to embody the truth.
Some have called Buddhism "a true warrior's religion" because of this aspect of self-reliance.

The Nature Of A "Buddha"

The reason we are all able to achieve Enlightenment is that every living being — even "lower" creatures, such as insects — has what is known as "Buddha nature".

The ability to achieve enlightenment lies in our consciousness – the ability of our minds to see the truth and practice living according to that truth.

Because every sentient being contains the living force, and perceives that it is alive, every sentient being has a Buddha nature, or the seed of enlightenment.

From Buddha's perspective, all the negative influences – greed, selfishness, ignorance– can be reduced and eliminated from the mind.

As the Dalai Lama explained in an interview:

*"There is no reason to believe some sentient being cannot become Buddha.
Every sentient being has that seed."*

Buddhism Today

Two and a half millennia after Buddha lived, nearly 500 million people worldwide now practice some form of Buddhism.

In every country in Asia, as well as many places in Europe and America, people practice different forms of Buddhism that vary from the original Indian tradition.

In every area – from China to Vietnam, Japan and the U.S. – core Buddhist teachings are adapted, to some degree, to the existing culture. Some strains of Buddhism are highly theoretical, while others are more focused on ritual and practice.

Chapter 2:
The Words Of The Buddha

"I reached in experience the Nirvana which is unborn, unrivalled, secure from attachment, undecaying and unstained.

This condition is indeed reached by me which is deep, difficult to see, difficult to understand, tranquil, excellent, beyond the reach of mere logic, subtle, and to be realized only by the wise."

- Buddha

The Buddha's teaching was initially simply oral; he described his insights and guidance to the followers who were his contemporaries.

He taught for 45 years, adapting the teachings to suit the students he was addressing. The language he used is understood to be Magadhi, an old language from eastern India.

Today, there are spoken and written traditions that have evolved over time to include the wisdom and writings of Buddha's disciples, as well as the words of Buddha himself.

Oral Tradition

While the Buddha lived, many of his teachings were memorized by one of his cousins and closest followers, Ven. (Venerable) Ananda, among others.

After the Buddha died (around 480 BCE), Buddha's followers, including Ven. Ananda and other monks, convened a council – known now as the First Council.

The Buddha's teachings were recited, discussed and

authenticated by this group. From this point forward, an established, reliable oral tradition within the spiritual community of monks ensured his teachings were accurately passed down.

At special occasions, festivals and within circles of disciples, the teachings of the Buddha were recited and referred to, and communicated down to generations of new followers.

It is because of the origins in oral communication that the authenticated teachings, whether spoken or written, starts with the words "Evam me sutam" — "Thus have I heard." This historic oral tradition continues even today.

The Sangha – the spiritual community of monks – chant selected sutras or teachings at ceremonies. Sometimes, the broader Buddhist community outside the monastery also joins in.

In addition to communicating the Buddha's teachings, chanting these canonical texts is considered to be a sacred act.

Written Tradition

After three more Councils of the Buddhist community had been held, the Fourth Council, which took place in Sri Lanka in approximately 25 BCE, oversaw the writing of the first written texts, recorded in the Pali language.

The writing was done through a process of etching on dried palm leaves with a metal stylus. When ink was then rubbed over the etchings, the writing became clear and durable.

To tie the pages together and keep them in order, a thread was passed through the pages. Beautifully-painted wooden covers secured the books, and protected them from wear.

The written language used in the canonical texts, Pali, is a relative of Magadhi, the language spoken in central India during the Buddha's time.

Of course, we cannot confirm that the Pali Canon contains the actual words uttered by Siddartha Gautama himself. Furthermore, as with many ancient prophets, there are plenty of reasons to question the historical accuracy of many parts of the written testimony.

Nevertheless, the core principles in these writings have served for centuries as an indispensable guide for millions of followers in their quest for enlightenment.

What Are the Sutras?

The Buddhist canon consists of discourses, or religious literature, called the Sutras — the words and teachings of the Buddha.

These are the "measuring stick" by which other writings are judged. They contain the core Buddhist teachings that other texts further illuminate and elaborate upon.

In contemporary collections of Buddhist writings, there are hundreds of sutras to be found. There are more than a thousand extremely influential Buddhist texts in various languages – including well-known Sutras such as The Lotus Sutra, The Heart Sutra and

The Diamond Sutra. These provide additional teachings, guidance on behavior and conduct, and commentary on various states after death in the progression to Nirvana.

The Pali Canon, which means "the word of Buddha," includes some of the Buddha's discourse, and also incorporates the teachings of his followers and students.

Many well-known Buddhist texts are actually not found in the Pali Canon, but are nonetheless considered part of the core literature.

As you will see, different traditions of Buddhism follow canonical and noncanonical literature to different degrees.

Pali Canon

In a wider sense, the Pali Canon is considered to be all the records of the Buddha's life. The whole Buddhist canon contains writings from a number of spiritual leaders over the 2,500 years since the Buddha's incarnation.

The canon contains hundreds of documents, with thousands upon thousands of pages. There, you will find wisdom, insights and poetic commentary from generations of Buddhist monks and scholars.

It includes works such as The Dhammapada, The Diamond Sutra, and The Tibetan Book of the Dead.

The Pali Canon comprise writings organized into three "baskets": The Sutta Pitaka, Vinaya Pitaka, and Abidharma Pitaka.

- The Sutta Pitaka consists of the main teachings of the Buddha or Dharma. This basket is further divided into five collections or Nikayas, depending on the subject matter discussed and the length of the discourses.

    These collections include the long teachings, medium length teachings, and groups of shorter teachings concerning common topics.

- The Vinaya Pitaka contains the 227 rules of conduct and discipline that apply to Buddhist monks and nuns. The rules are clearly stated, and the context for their origination is explained.

- The Abhidamma Pitaka consists of seven books, and includes a philosophical analysis of the teaching. This seems to be a product of the monks' clarifications of the Sutta Pikaya and Vinaya Pitaka in the earlier days.

The Councils have checked and agreed upon the Pali Canon over the course of centuries, and it has been translated into countless different languages across the world.

Dharma & "The Four Reliances"

There is no single-word translation for the word "dharma" in the Indian religious traditions. In Buddhism, dharma refers to the right way of living, the truths or laws of existence, as well as the teachings of the Buddha.

While the word 'dharma' contains many ideas, its most important meaning is arguably "the unmediated truth" (as experienced by the enlightened mind). This implies that Buddha's words are not the only dharma, or source of dharma.

A short and simple Sutra called the "Four Reliances Sutra", provides some guidance as to how people are meant to understand the sources of truth that can lead directly to enlightenment.

The Four Reliances Sutra

According to Buddhism, the four things we should have reliance on are:

1. The Dharma.

2. The true meanings.

3. The suttas whose meaning is clear.

4. Wisdom, or extraordinary knowledge.

Each of these elements becomes clearer when considered in contrast to things we should not rely on.

Let us go through them one by one.

1. Reliance on the Dharma:
   > This simply means that you should rely on the truth or the principle, not only on the person teaching it.
   >
   > If you understand the principle, then you can apply it on your own, even without the immediate commentary or guidance from the person.
   >
   > No human being is perfect – but the principles can be. A teacher could inadvertently lead you astray, but the principles never will.

2. Reliance on the true meanings:
   > Rely on the significance of a teaching, not just the literal words. See past the words to the actual meaning behind them.
   >
   > People can apply authoritative words in such a strict way that may not be quite right.
   >
   > There may be more than one way to describe the truth.

Once you understand the meaning, you can see what is right in different descriptions.

Adherence to the original wording may get in the way of a person truly understanding the significance of a teaching.

3. Reliance on the suttas whose meaning is already clear:

Sometimes, you read Sutras and you do not understand it. If so, you can consult other translations to see if you can penetrate the meaning of it from different perspectives. If not, you should leave it be, at least for the moment.

4. Reliance on wisdom:

Have confidence in your wisdom – not just in your thinking. Thinking can be linear and limited.

Sometimes, you can see the whole picture through direct knowledge, instead of spending precious time putting the puzzle pieces together one by one.

As is often the case, the more you think about deep subjects, the more confused you get.

Maybe you were thinking along the wrong lines, going off on a tangent and losing track of the big picture, yet you keep rationalizing to yourself that it's correct.

Buddha himself understands this possibility quite well, as is apparent in his discourse at the village of Kalama, relayed to us in the Kalama Sutta...

The Kalama Sutta, or Kalama Discourse

"Believe nothing merely because you have been told it. Do not believe what your teacher tells you merely out of respect for the teacher.

But whatsoever, after due examination and analysis, you find to be kind, conducive to the good, the benefit, the welfare of all beings — that doctrine, believe and cling to, and take it as your guide."
- Buddha

The Kalama Sutta describes an event in which Buddha passes through the village of Kesaputta. As Buddha arrives at the village, he is greeted by the villagers, a clan called the Kalamas. They tell him that many wandering ascetics have passed through their village recently.

Each one, the villagers say, criticizes the teachings of others, and tries to explain why their own teaching is the best. How, they ask the Buddha, can they know whose teachings they should adopt and follow? In response, the Buddha takes time to speak to the group, and his words are captured in what has become known as the Kalama Sutta.

Do not simply believe the teachings of the wandering monks, he tells the Kalamas, just because they are claimed to be true.

A person can see for him or herself whether the teachings are correct, based on one's own state of anxiety and suffering.

Buddha encourages the Kalamas to listen to the words of wise men. However, he notes that they should consider these words in their everyday lives, so they, themselves, can discern what is useful.

The Kalama Sutta states:
- Do not act upon what has been acquired by repeated hearing
- nor upon tradition
- nor upon rumor
- nor upon what is in a scripture

- nor upon surmise
- nor upon an axiom
- nor upon specious reasoning
- nor upon a bias towards a notion that has been pondered over
- nor upon another's seeming ability
- nor upon the idea of, 'the monk is our teacher'.

In conclusion, the Buddha explains that when they have tested and learned from their experience, and observed the positive results in their own lives, they will know which teachings merit respect and practice. The instruction of the Kalama Sutta is thus famous for its encouragement of free inquiry.

The sutta teaches principles that are opposed to dogmatism, authoritarianism and intolerance. Thus, the Kalama Sutta is at the core of the Buddha's mandate to seek the truth evidenced in one's own experience.

Balance

In pursuit of enlightenment and release from suffering, there must be a balance in seeking the truth. Wisdom of the Enlightened One and others guides us, and provides stepping stones on the way. Yet, blind adherence to any of these can become an impediment to seeing truth.

Because we all have Buddha nature in us, we are all capable of attaining this truth without reliance on tampered words, rules or gurus.

In addition, the teachings are meant to be practical, and to palpably relieve one's suffering by guiding towards true thoughts and wise actions.

With this in mind, we can each judge whether we are being led in the right direction by our own experience and judgement, and/or by mentors and teachings.

It's important to note, however, that the Kalama Sutta is not intended to support extreme skepticism, the notion of radical subjectivism or the imagination of an individual truth.

Instead, the intention is to emphasize the way that

the three poisons – greed, anger and delusion – could lead one astray.

Furthermore, it encourages seekers to accept wisdom, and work to verify the important principles through their own experiential results.

Consequently, one should gain perspective on one's own thoughts and motivations to move away from actions motivated by these three poisons.

Moral judgements of actions can therefore be deduced by analyzing whether these actions are based on unwholesome origins or not.

What is the Abhidharma?

The Abhidharma is the third part of the Pali Canon. The writings in this collection are more theoretical and philosophical than in the other two portions. It provides a conceptual framework for the insights revealed in the Sutta Pitaka.

The Abhidharma delves into the importance of

intentionality within the Buddhist framework — it is the intention behind an action that primarily determines its karmic potential.
In the Abhidharma discourses, a wide variety of human mental states are discussed and analyzed.

It explains how a person can create positive and negative karmic thoughts by paying attention to one's own mental state.

Some say that understanding the Dharma through the knowledge gained from the Sutta Pitaka alone, is like trying to understand human health by studying the remedies for various illnesses.

While understanding remedies is important, having a conceptual, big-picture understanding of health, and what kinds of imbalances cause illness, is a much more powerful way of understanding.

With this kind of knowledge, one can better teach about different ways to preserve and restore health and, by analogy, the Dharma and truth.

A person who has studied the Abhidharma can more

thoroughly grasp the nature of the mind, and gain insight into many related truths and illusions, skillful and unskillful actions.

Chapter 3: Different Traditions

Buddhism – like all other major world religions – has evolved with time, experience and geographical dispersion.

As with the other traditions, natural groupings develop according to the extent to which believers adhere to original teachings and core texts, and how much they rely on the authority of the monks, priests or rabbis.

Examples from other religions may be helpful in understanding the general outlines of the major traditions in Buddhism: Theravada, Mahayana and Vajrayana.

- Within each major world religion, some traditions consider themselves to be the most conservative and true to the original prophet's intention (Theravada).

- Others believe that interpreting the original writings in the spirit of modern life, and adapting those teachings according to new insights and evolving social norms, is preferable (Mahayana).

- Some even blend beliefs and traditions that were already present in indigenous societies, together with the teachings of the more mainstream religious orders (Vajrayana).

When we look at the overall makeup of modern Buddhism across all its branches, Theravada Buddhists account for approximately 36 percent of practitioners, Mahayana accounts for around 53 percent, while Vajrayana and other smaller groups make up the remaining 10 or so percent.

Theravada

The word "Theravada" is derived from the Pali language, and is a combination of the words thera (meaning "elders") and vada (meaning "word, doctrine"). So, simply stated, Theravada Buddhism is known as the "Doctrine of the Elders".

It is most closely tied to the Pali Canon, or Tipitaka, which is generally regarded as the oldest record of the Buddha's teachings.

It is generally accepted that Theravada Buddhism is closest to the original form and practice. From Siddartha Gautama's original home in the mountains of northern India (modern day Bihar), groups of followers formed and developed a sturdy tradition.

In spite of the strong appeal of Buddhist teachings to many, the dominant religion of Hinduism remained firmly in place in most of India. Today, there are estimated to be no more than 8 million practicing Buddhists in India, compared to 4 million Jains, 21 million Sihks and 24 million Christians.

As adherents spread the wisdom and guiding principles of the Buddha to the north — first into Cambodia, Vietnam and China and then a few centuries later into Korea and Japan — the teachings of disciples were incorporated into the main "canon" of texts, and the emphasis on personal experience grew.

Theravada Buddhism became the primary religion in sections of Southeast Asia, including Sri Lanka, Burma, and Thailand. Today, more than 100 million people world-wide practice Theravada Buddhism.

As you've probably noticed, in recent decades, many people in Western countries have been drawn to Buddhist teachings. There are now significant numbers of practicing Buddhists in these areas as well.

Theravada Buddhism is centered on strict individual meditation, and maintains that the path to

Enlightenment is through the life of an ascetic monk, which allows near-complete detachment from the sources of suffering. Mahayana Buddhism offers the hope of freedom to laypeople as well.

In addition, Mahayana encourages what is known as the "Bodhisattva ideal" in which Awakened ones work to save all beings with Buddha nature from the cycle of death and rebirth.

The Many Names of Buddhism

Over the many centuries, various names for Theravada Buddhism have sprung forth.

During his lifetime, the Buddha himself referred to his teachings as Dharma Vinaya, "the truth/doctrine" and "the education/discipline". Theravada – the doctrine of the elders – adheres most closely and exclusively to these earliest teachings.

Because Theravada Buddhism is so prevalent in Southeast Asia (Sri Lanka, Thailand, and Burma), it is often referred to as "Southern Buddhism."

On the other hand, "Northern Buddhism" refers to the forms that were adopted in regions such as Tibet, China, Japan, and Korea.

Another set of terms uses the Sanskrit word "yana" which means "vehicle". For example, Theravada is sometimes called "Hinayana", the "Lesser Vehicle", while "Mahayana" is known as the "Greater Vehicle."

Originally, the term Hinayana was meant pejoratively, because it was used primarily by northern monks who adhered more closely to the form of Buddhism that has become known as Mahayana.

Today, however, scholars of Buddhism often use the term Hinayana without any disparaging connotations.

Mahayana Buddhism is more or less a blanket term that refers to many schools found in Northern Buddhism, including Tibetan Buddhism, Ch'an Buddhism in China and Japanese Zen.

The third major grouping of Buddhist schools is

known as "Vajrayana." "Vajra" means "thunderbolt" or "diamond" in Sanskrit, and Vajrayana is known as the Diamond Vehicle or Thunderbolt Vehicle. Because Vajrayana Buddhism was the latest to develop historically, it has fewer practitioners than the dominant schools.

Of course, as with many other religions, there are many fine distinctions within the different schools. The names of other smaller groupings often come from a certain aspect of Buddha's teachings they choose to emphasize.

For example, Vajrayana Buddhists are considered part of a grouping of "Mantrayana", schools which seek the path to enlightenment through use of mantras in meditation.

The differences in the naming of these schools of thought also have implications for some of their beliefs. For example, one school of Buddhism teaches that it takes three incalculable eons for a soul to reach Buddhahood. Others claim that Buddhahood is achievable in a single lifetime.

These are just a few examples that highlight the differences in interpretation that separate the schools of Buddhism.

The Buddha's Teachings

Theravada Buddhism draws its core guidance from the canonical texts, meant to be the Buddha's own words on doctrine and discipline (beliefs and practice), which are written in the Pali language.

Hence the term "Pali Canon". The essence of Buddhist teaching lies at the heart of every form of Buddhist tradition.

Shortly after his enlightenment under the Bodhi tree, the Buddha delivered his first discourse, in which he laid out the essential foundation for all of his subsequent teachings.

This foundation consists of the Four Noble Truths — four fundamental principles of nature that became clear when the Buddha's awakened to the true nature of existence.

As touched upon earlier, Buddha does not convey these truths as articles of faith to be taken on authority, but rather as an accurate description of lived existence, which can be verified in each person's own experience of life.

Again, the Four Noble Truths are as follows:

1. Life is fundamentally characterized by suffering and disappointment;

2. The cause of this suffering is tanha (craving) in all its forms;

3. Suffering can be relieved through abandoning craving;

4. There is a method of achieving the end of all unsatisfactoriness, namely the Noble Eightfold Path.

The Buddha taught his followers about the Noble Eightfold Path and how they could begin to approach enlightenment.

The first steps along the path involve the development of the foundations for a good life. The good life is based on truth, or more specifically, right speech, right action, and right livelihood.

Next, he taught the development of right effort, right mindfulness, and right concentration — or samadhi.

The final step is the development of panna, or wisdom, which includes the right view and right resolve.

Through all the steps it is important to cultivate the spirit and practice generosity (dana), as this helps develop a compassionate heart and balances out unskillful tendencies towards attachment.

Progress along the path is iterative, and the steps are mutually reinforcing. The development of each aspect of the Noble Eightfold Path deepens one's insight into, and capacity to develop, the others. This then leads the practitioner forward in a path toward eventual enlightenment.

The emphasis in Theravada Buddhism is on the

importance of a monastic life, following a gradual path, the iterative strengthening of mind, as well as practice and wisdom.

This stands in sharp relief when contrasted with Zen Buddhism's belief in the "moment of enlightenment" — the possibility of a sudden enlightenment without an extended build-up period.

Mahayana

Mahayana Buddhism now accounts for the majority of Buddhists in the world. The primary difference between Mahayana Buddhism and Theravada Buddhism lies in the Mahayana belief that even non-monks can reach enlightenment.

The goal of spiritual Buddhist practice in both the Mahayana and Vajrayana traditions is to reach closer to enlightenment — to become a Bodhisattva, and to be reincarnated as a higher being.

A Bodhisattva is called a "fully enlightened Buddha", and can lead followers to enlightenment. They can aid other beings with Buddha nature in achieving relief from suffering and, eventually, their own awakening.

The goal of practice for the Mahayana tradition is for individuals to reach enlightenment in this lifetime — becoming an arhat, a 'perfected person' – and not to be reincarnated again.

As mentioned, Mahayana Buddhists teach that one does not need to be an ascetic Buddhist monk to reach enlightenment, and that a person can attain awakening in a single lifetime – rather than over eons.

This belief has its roots in Buddha's teachings about the Buddha nature, and can be seen in his discourse at Kalama – conveyed to us in the Kalamata Sutta.

This particular discourse emphasized the degree to which individuals must be open to sources of wisdom and authority – e.g. mentors and the sutras – while they must also validate this guidance and practice with their own experience and judgment.

Over several centuries, Mahayana Buddhism – "Southern Buddhism" spread from India to various other South, East and Southeast Asian from Bangladesh and Nepal across Asia to Malaysia and Singapore.

The "Greater Vehicle" now has practitioners in every Asian country, and is the largest of the three schools of Buddhism.

Vajrayana

Vajrayana, (translated as "Thunderbolt Vehicle" or "Diamond Vehicle") is a form of Buddhism that incorporates more diverse elements from other cultures. The most famous branch of Vajrayana in the West is what we call Tibetan Buddhism.

It should be noted that some scholars classify Vajrayana as part of the Mahayana school, while others consider it a separate branch. A portion also argue that Tibetan Buddhism is a special case, and cannot be rightly classified as part of the Vajrayana tradition.

Regardless of its overall classification, it can be agreed upon that Vajrayana represents a change in the way Buddhist ideas are incorporated into the everyday life of individuals.

Tibetan Buddhism represents a blend of classic Buddhism together with yoga and tantric practices. Towards the end of the eighth century, the first influences of Buddhism can be seen in India's close neighbor, Tibet.

About five hundred years later, there was another large wave of Buddhist influence there, as well. The form of Buddhism that migrated into Tibet had already blended Hindu tantric practices and yoga together the classical teachings of the Buddha.

A key difference between the way Vajrayana and the other traditions approach the life of the layperson is the importance placed on rituals.

Whereas Theravada emphasizes the need to lead a monastic life in order to attain enlightenment, the Vajrayana teaches that including the appropriate rites is an essential element of being on the path to becoming a Boddhisatva.

Tibetan Buddhism acknowledges that there are two paths to enlightenment.
One path is grounded in the canonical teachings, and is based on compassion, meditation, emptiness and truth.

The other path blends the Buddha's teachings with everyday rituals that address the practical, as well as spiritual aspects, of human life, including yoga and tantra.

To conclude this chapter about the different branches of Buddhism, consider the following quote by Dalai Lama about the Heart Sutra:

"It is very important to understand that the core teachings of the Theravada tradition embodied in the Pali scriptures are the foundation of the Buddha's teachings.

Beginning with these teachings, one can then draw on the insights contained in the detailed explanations of the Sanskrit Mahayana tradition.

Finally, integrating techniques and perspectives from the Vajrayana texts can further enhance one's understanding. But without a foundation in the core teachings embodied in the Pali tradition, simply proclaiming oneself a follower of the Mahayana is meaningless.

If one has this kind of deeper understanding of various scriptures and their interpretation, one is spared from harboring mistaken notions of conflicts between the "Greater" versus the "Lesser" Vehicle.

Sometimes, there is a regrettable tendency on the part of certain followers of the Mahayana to disparage the teachings of the Theravada, claiming that they are the teachings of the Lesser Vehicle, and thereby not suited to one's own personal practice.

Similarly, on the part of followers of the Pali tradition, there is sometimes a tendency to reject the validity of the Mahayana teachings, claiming they are not actually the Buddha's teachings.

As we move into our examination of the Heart Sutra, what is important is to understand deeply how these traditions complement each other, and to see how, at the individual level, each of us can integrate all these core teachings into our personal practice."

Chapter 4: The Three Marks of Existence & The Four Noble Truths

"The world is afflicted by death and decay. But the wise do not grieve, having realized the nature of the world."

- Buddha

To gain a complete view of things, the Buddhist teachings and practices must be understood in the

context of a Buddhist view of existence.
The Three Marks of Existence are:

- Impermanence (Annica)

- Not-Self (Dukka)

- Suffering (Anatta)

1. Impermanence
The first of the three marks of existence can be understood as a rough equivalent of our modern saying that "the only constant is change".

In the Buddhist worldview, this applies to every single thing in the universe. Everything is changing – even stars and rocks – though we usually fail to appreciate the change that is occurring all around us.

Human beings often believe they want all good things – situations, achievements, our health, relationships – to be permanent. We create something, we want it to stay that way, and we believe it *should* stay that way.

We become upset when things change, because it seems to violate our fundamental sense of how things should be in the world. It is not fair that things we enjoy and count on do not last. Due to this perception, we experience suffering.

Buddhists believe that once we recognize that impermanence/change is the true nature of everything we experience, we begin to experience the world and our lives differently. Our suffering is lessened when we understand and accept that change is just how everything is.

It is difficult to not want the things that bring us joy to continue – but we are able to better let go and cope with change once we are able to recognize the truth of impermanence.

2. Not-Self

The second of the three marks – Not-Self – can seem less obvious than impermanence. Not-Self, however, is simply an extension and application of the idea of impermanence to the idea of who we are as individuals.

One way to think of Not-Self is see it as a teaching that shows us the limits of ourselves, and who we believe we are.

For example, it is important to recognize that we are not the same as our bodies. Of course, we identify with our bodies in many ways, for better or worse.

However, if we get a haircut, we are still the same person. If we break a tooth, we are still the same person. If we lose a limb or an organ, we may relate to our bodies differently, but this physical change does not change the essence of who we are.

Similarly, we have beliefs about ourselves such as "I am a man", "I am a woman", "I am 40 years old" etc. These ideas seem to imply a sense of permanence about characteristics we associate with these labels.

However, as with physical changes, we see that, in fact, none of these aspects of ourselves are truly definitive of who we are.

We think, feel and change constantly. Becoming too

attached to certain beliefs about "who we are" – or are not – can be a source of suffering, because it blinds us to the truth of continuous change.
At a biological level, we are also everchanging.

Our cells and physical processes work, adapt and build. We become more mature, stronger, wiser, older and then begin to decline physically – yet none of this is permanent. None of it defines us.

We can recognize the limits of these ways of thinking of ourselves, and rather observe existence through this new lens of truth. This allows us to free ourselves from many sources of suffering.

3. Suffering

The third mark of existence is very closely related to the first of the Four Noble Truths. Suffering is part of existence as a human being. Each of us suffer as an individual, and those around us are also suffering, each in his or her own way.

Human beings spend much of their time trying to avoid recognizing that they suffer. They want to persist in their beliefs that happiness and achievement can be attained and made permanent.

In spite of evidence to the contrary all around us, it can seem that it is easier to chase permanence than to accept the impermanence of everything. It can be profoundly disorienting to realize that the foundations of your efforts in life are not what you believed they were.

In addition, recognizing that the state of existence inherently involves suffering also leads to compassion for other living beings. Understanding the nature of suffering at a deep level is the key to being able to release oneself from it.

> *"See them, floundering in their sense of mine, like fish in the puddles of a dried-up stream – and, seeing this, live with no mine, not forming attachment for states of becoming."*
>
> - Buddha

Buddha described the Four Noble Truths of human existence (mentioned in Chapter 1) as an initial mental framework to understand suffering in the context of the three marks of existence.

The first Noble Truth is the reality of dukkha, or suffering, as part of being.

The word "dukkha" plays a central role in Buddhism. It means "that which is difficult to bear". It can be understood as suffering, stress, discomfort, pain, or anxiety.

None of these words quite capture the meaning of dukkha, however. The original word symbolizes a full range of experiences, from subtle inner conflicts, to physical pain and existential despair. As it's the most versatile, we will use the common translation: "suffering".

The second Noble Truth is that Dukkha is caused by desiring permanence, and falsely clinging to the notion that Self is permanent. One must comprehend that existence entails suffering. One must recognize the causes of suffering – attachment and craving.

The third Noble Truth is Nirvana. One must

realize that suffering can cease. Beyond attachment, craving, control and existence is Nirvana. The realization of Nirvana is supreme awakening, or Bodhi.

Attaining this awakening is the goal of Buddhist practice. Essentially, it means awakening to the way things *really* are – to the fundamental truths of the universe. It is waking up to our true Buddha nature.

Mahayana teachings discuss Nirvana in more detailed ways than Theravada does. Attaining Nirvana is described in various ways in the ancient writings – it is sometimes called attaining one's original mind, or one's Buddha nature.

It can also be described as seeing infinite light and infinite life. No words can fully convey Nirvana, however, as it is beyond space and time.

The fourth Noble Truth is that there is an Eightfold Path to enlightenment. From our perspective, the path is a paradox.

Awakening is not created by anything;

enlightenment, your true nature, is already present. We are simply not aware of this reality. In other words, we do not know what we do not know.

The Noble Eightfold Path shows us the way to relief from suffering and to our eventual release, once and for all, from samsara — the cycle of suffering and rebirth in which we have been bound for countless eons.

The Eightfold Path shows us the different aspects of a completely pure and enlightened life, one that is "right" in all the significant aspects of human life – from livelihood to mindfulness.

These qualities will be discussed in more detail in the next chapter, when we introduce Buddhist notions of reincarnation, karma, Nirvana, the Buddhist cosmology, and the way of thinking and feeling that impedes our ability to follow the Eightfold Path and attain Nirvana.

Chapter 5: Buddhist Cosmology

The idea of Impermanence as one of the Three Marks of Existence applies to the whole Buddhist conception of the nature and origins of the universe.

As an introduction, it is fair to say that the Buddhist conception of the universe extends to unimaginable lengths in both time and space. The cosmos comprises countless layers of complexity – with "worlds", "realms", "abodes", "heavens", "earthly realms", "hells (cold and hot ones)", "boddhisatva", and "Buddha" levels, among many others.

The roots of this complex cosmology lie in the Hindu origins of Buddhism itself, and were augmented and developed by a number of different thinkers through the millennia. Exceedingly complex distinctions exist within each part – like a giant fractal.

Multidimensional Faith

Scholars describe Buddhist cosmology in two pieces: spatial and temporal. The spatial cosmology is in turn described in terms of vertical and horizontal dimensions.

The vertical cosmology describes a hierarchy of "planes of existence", in which all of life takes place, according to the level of spiritual evolution of the beings in question.

In total there are thirty-one planes of existence, and the planes are grouped into three realms each corresponding to a different type of mentality.

There is an Earthly Realm within this complex system of planes of existence – and all human life takes place in a physical location on the Earth within this Earthly Realm.

The temporal cosmology of Buddhism clearly reflects its Hindu origins. The universe is believed to be infinitely old, and that it continues infinitely into the future. In keeping with the three marks of existence, everything in the universe is impermanent and continually changes in a cyclical fashion.

The context of the infinite Buddhist cosmos is significant. The unfathomable magnitude of the eons of time, as well as the countless realms, serve to underscore the transient nature of the illusions we often cling to.

Within the cosmos, beings die and are reborn countless times, cycling through samsara – the wheel of existence.

Because our Buddha nature is timeless, it naturally follows that the physical forms our essence takes will change with each manifestation of a lifetime. The nature of the cycles of evolution in the universe are not seen as random, but follow more or less clear laws of karmic energy.

As the Buddha meditated under the Bodhi tree, he eventually recognized all of his past lives, and then the past lives of others. In the end, he gained perfect knowledge of this world and the worlds beyond it — he was enlightened.

Karmic Cycles

According to Buddhist beliefs, this force of spiritual nature, or karma, is affected positively or negatively by the feelings and actions of conscious beings. Buddhist cosmology is fueled, in a sense, by karma.

Good and bad actions – or skillful and unskillful actions, as Buddhists prefer to think of them – create good or bad karma, respectively.

In each life, a soul is subject to the effects of the karma it has created, in the current life as well as in earlier ones. This spiritual energy comes back to each person, either as experiences in this life, or as consequences in future lives. The Buddhist belief in karma creates part of the rationale for living a good, moral life full of compassion.

"Just as a mother would protect her only child with her life, even so let one cultivate a boundless love towards all beings."

- Buddha

It is important to note that the way karma works is not like the punishments or rewards of a deity. Karma is impersonal; it is simply a natural law — the way things are.

The best outcome for suffering souls is to be able to escape samara — the karmic cycle of death and rebirth – and reach Nirvana, which is the highest spiritual point of existence, and the end of the self.

Nirvana is Sanskrit for "to extinguish", and implies that in Nirvana, ignorance, hatred and earthly suffering are all eliminated.

Chapter 6:
The Five Skandhas

The Buddhist concept of the five skandhas, or "aggregates," underlies much of Buddhist practice of self-cultivation – seeking enlightenment along the Eightfold Path.

The ideals of Buddhist ethics include how people ought to interact with one another — what is considered 'skillful' action and thoughts. These are based in the concept of self, and are illuminated by being contrasted with the skandhas.

The skandhas are essentially illusions about a person's own identity. The fundamental insight to gain from the teaching of the five skandhas, is that these illusions do not give you identity — they are not identical with, or part of, you.

They are temporary mental and physical aspects, as well as habits, that can be conflated with the notion of a Self, but none of them represents what a being truly is.

The five skandhas include one physical and four mental factors:

1. Body (rupa)

2. Feelings (vedana), or sensations of all kinds.

3. Perceptions (sanna).

4. Formations (sankhara), or automatic thought processes.

5. Sense consciousness (vinnana).

The Buddha taught that clinging to these skandhas or aggregates as "me" is to give into illusion – and thus leads to suffering.

Our notion of a permanent selfhood is based on these five aggregates. We are them, and they are us. They bring about our thoughts, feelings, ideas, evaluations and attitudes that filter and create our experience.

They change from moment to moment; they are not static, but continuously evolve. Because they build and filter our world, and because they entail suffering, our world (but not necessarily *the* world) involves suffering as well.

The Buddha explained that subduing cravings for these five skandhas is beneficial. This is because when they change or alter, as they inevitably do, there will be no stress or upset to weigh you down.

As we examine each skandha in turn, we see that we are not identical with it – it does not define us, and is not essential for us to be "who we are".

When we realize the skandhas are only temporary

phenomena, we are on the path to enlightenment, because we have more profoundly understood the mark of existence that is Not-Self.

The Four Solaces

The Kalama Sutta contains what are known as Buddha's four solaces. These solaces are Buddha's assertion that moral life would be correct, and would relieve suffering, even if there were no karma and reincarnation.

Even if good actions are not rewarded good outcomes, and bad actions with bad outcomes, we can still perceive the truth of pursuing mindful awakening and skillful action.

Consider this discourse by the Buddha, from the Kalama Sutta:

"Suppose there is a hereafter and there is a fruit, result, of deeds done well or ill.
Then, it is possible that at the dissolution of the body after death, I shall arise in the heavenly world,

which is possessed of the state of bliss.'

This is the first solace found by him.

Suppose there is no hereafter and there is no fruit, no result, of deeds done well or ill. Yet in this world, here and now, free from hatred, free from malice, safe and sound, and happy, I keep myself.'

This is the second solace found by him.

Suppose evil befall an evil-doer. I, however, think of doing evil to no one. Then, how can ill affect me who do no evil deed?'

This is the third solace found by him.

Suppose evil do not befall an evil-doer. Then I see myself purified in any case.'

This is the fourth solace found by him."

According to these teachings, a person with a pure mind will find clarity, contentment and peace in these four solaces.

These four solaces show us that the imperative to live a life of loving-kindness and compassion does not depend on belief in Buddhist cosmology, karma and reincarnation.

The mental well-being and perspective gained through appreciation of impermanence and skillful action is enough to provide solace.

Chapter 7: The Three Poisons & The Three Jewels

As you now know, according to Buddhist teachings, human suffering is caused by attachment to attributes of the five skandhas – which blinds us to the true nature of reality (the three marks of existence). This blindness leads to greed, anger and ignorance.

The Three Poisons

Greed, anger and ignorance are known as "The Three Poisons". They are the symptoms of our lack of understanding of reality, and our attachment to possessions, image of Self, and the notion of permanence. Furthermore, they create additional energy and momentum towards even more attachment and suffering.

We can see examples of this all around us — stress, competition, materialism, obesity, and indifference to the plight of others. These are just a few examples of what Buddhists would see as evidence of the three poisons at work.

The Buddha describes greed, anger and ignorance as hindrances, bonds and knots. These poisons fill our lives with pain and unhappiness. They lead us to make bad decisions, which affect our karmic energy and our future. They cause us to have selfish intentions.

Because our intentions are selfish, we are dishonest about them, and we tend to act unethically and immorally. In this way, the three poisons cause us pain on a personal level, and then translate to many of the ills of our society.

The karma created by actions based in these poisons keeps us in an endless cycle of death and rebirth.

The Four Noble Truths teach us that when we understand and embrace the causes of our anxiety and suffering – by first recognizing impermanence – we can then learn to accept the way things truly are, and begin the process of seeking enlightenment.

Greed

Our greed and jealousy are like a burning thirst, a ravenous craving, and unappeasable lust. We feel we need the objects of our desire to complete us in some way — to provide us with lasting satisfaction. We mistakenly believe our happiness is dependent upon achieving that goal.

However, when we attain the goal, we are not satisfied and not complete – so we seek another goal. Once again, we will look outside of ourselves for the next big thing that will make us happy.

We cannot rest; we believe we just need more accomplishment, more material objects, more admiration and love. This leads to another common symptom of our greed.

Caught up in the cycle of craving and greed, we often ignore other people, and forget to show compassion. We become suspicious and jealous in relationships.

Our greed, jealousy, craving, and lack of generosity affects each of us on a personal level, creating social and global issues as a result. It can be an endless, vicious cycle that never leads to contentedness and peace.

Anger

The poison of anger is the emotional source of destructiveness, vengefulness, intolerance, dislike and hatred. Anger can lead us into a vicious cycle. We may feel that most people are against us, and we seek or create conflict in many areas of our lives.

When there is conflict, or perceived threats around us, we think constantly about how we can protect ourselves, and how to get back at those who compete with us.

This stress, fear and anger in turn leads us to reject and repress our own inner feelings of hatred, hurt, fear and alienation. We treat these feelings like an internal enemy. With the poison of anger, we harm ourselves, create conflict and push others away.

Ignorance

Ignorance is the poison rooted in our wrong understanding of reality — we are not in harmony with the way existence is truly structured.

Affected by the poison of ignorance, we do not understand that all life is interdependent, interconnected and impermanent. Thus, we constantly misconstrue our problems, and what would actually bring us satisfaction.

We look outward for a better partner, a better job, a different city, or circumstances that will finally give us relief and make us happy.

Because of our ignorance, we do not understand how we can find or create true happiness. We do not understand that the direction in which we need to search is inward.

As a result, we fail to understand the negative and unskillful actions that create suffering. This ignorance keeps us trapped in a vicious cycle from which we cannot escape.

The Three Jewels

Buddhism teaches us that the cycle of grasping for permanence must be slowed and reversed, as we turn our focus towards truth, compassion and enlightenment.

The "Three Jewels", or "Three Treasures", at the heart of Buddhism are:

1. The Buddha (the yellow jewel).

2. The Dharma (the blue jewel).

3. The Sangha (the red jewel).

By focusing our attention on these jewels, we slow the vicious cycle of the three poisons, and reverse it through our practice.

The Buddha

The yellow jewel, the Buddha, refers both to the ideal of Buddhahood and to Siddartha Gautama, the historical Buddha.

Adopting the ideal of the Buddha as your spiritual guiding light, and the example you seek to emulate, will help steer your daily practices to the truths he taught. It will lead you to seek release from suffering for yourself and all other beings.

The Dharma

As covered in the earlier chapters, the blue jewel— the Dharma — primarily means the truth the Buddha understood. The term Dharma in the context of the three jewels refers to the truth that Buddha articulated — that which is conveyed in the Buddhist tradition.

In other words, the teaching that the Buddha first put into words, and communicated to his followers and the first monks.

The first time he relayed this truth to his followers is traditionally referred to as 'the first turning of the wheel of the Dharma'. The Dharma wheel, with eight spokes, is a common symbol of Buddhism.

The Sangha
The red jewel is the Sangha – the spiritual community of teachers and practitioners around us.

Having conversation partners, fellow practitioners, and mentors to learn from, emulate and discuss things with can be essential to one's ability to pursue Buddhist practice and wisdom.

Since Buddhism is not only a belief, but a way of life, it is important that the tradition lives on in its community of practitioners.

The Sangha is a very broad term, and can be used to mean all Buddhists in the world, or even all

Buddhists who have ever lived.

Guided in the practice of loving kindness and compassion by these three jewels, the three poisons can be transformed into true happiness.

When we realize our interconnectedness and our oneness, we throw off the blinders that keep us from seeing the truth.

Chapter 8: The Five Precepts & The Eightfold Path

"It is wrong to think that misfortunes come from the east or from the west; they originate within one's own mind.

Therefore, it is foolish to guard against misfortunes from the external world, and leave the inner mind uncontrolled."

- Buddha

In Buddhism, there is much talk about 'skillful' and 'unskillful' actions and intentions. A mind that is skillful stays in harmony with the core truths of existence. Because of this, the actions that follow are unlikely to cause harm or suffering to others.

This terminology and its implications stands in stark contrast to the moral language of other major religions, such as Christianity, that characterize actions and states of mind as 'good' and 'evil'.

According to Buddhist teachings, what is skillful, ethical and desirable is an action that is likely to be positive for oneself and or for others.

On the other hand, unskillful and negative actions are those that are likely to be harmful to oneself or to others.

Moral conduct for Buddhists differs somewhat depending on whether one is a Buddhist monk, or simply a lay person living a normal life outside a monastery.

The Five Precepts

A lay, or non-monk, Buddhist follower should cultivate good habits of mind and body, by training in what are known as the "Five Precepts".

The five precepts are essentially training rules for integrating Buddhist teachings into one's way of being. If one fails to adhere to these rules, it is important to recognize the way in which one has failed, and learn how to avoid deviating from this guidance in the future.

In this way, a person trains his or her body and mind in the Buddhist way of interpreting and responding to existence.

It is helpful to highlight the contrast with, say, the ten commandments. If any of the ten commandments are broken, the actor will be considered guilty, and will be punished by God. Buddhism places the main emphasis on 'mind' instead.

Unskillful actions result in anxiety, guilt and remorse. A Buddhist seeks to avoid these unskillful actions and intentions, and instead develop right concentration on a peaceful state of mind

The five precepts are as follows:
1. To engage in the training to avoid taking the life of beings.

2. To engage in the training to avoid taking things that are not given.

3. To engage in the training to avoid sensual misconduct.

4. To engage in the training to refrain from speaking falsely.

5. To engage in the training to refrain from using substances that cause intoxication and heedlessness.

The Eightfold Path

Engaging in the training also means following the Eightfold Path that leads to Nirvana. This path involves focusing on improving yourself in eight essential areas of life: Concentration, views, speech,

resolve, action, livelihood, effort, mindfulness.
By doing this, you bring yourself into a state of being where you can accept impermanence and non-self.

The Eightfold Path is a paradox. This is because, on the one hand, the path should be followed, and when it is followed in such a way that it leads to clarity and balance in acceptance of the truth, it leads to enlightenment.

One the other hand, enlightenment can be seen as simply realizing a truth that is always present. Seen in this second way, enlightenment cannot be produced through any path or any other process, even the Buddha's teachings.

The challenge lies in the fact that we are not 'awake' to our true nature, even though it is always already present. The Eightfold Path is a set of aspects that you can, and should, focus on, if you are to live in harmony with the truth.

In following the Eightfold Path, we are slowly peeling back and letting go of our attachments, and learning to accept what is.

The Buddha recognized this paradox, and helped his followers understand the difference between the Eightfold Path and the truth that it leads to. He described his teaching as being like a raft.

If we need to get to the other side of a dangerous river, we may need to make a raft. It is essential to have in order to cross safely, and with it we can achieve our purpose – to get to the other side.

However, the raft is simply a "vehicle" – it gets us to where we want to go, but it is not the destination itself. In the same way, The Eightfold Path is a "vehicle", but it is not the truth or enlightenment. Once we are safely across the river, we do not need the raft any more.

In Buddha's analogy, this means we do not need to "cling" to the teachings. We rely on the teachings to get us where we need to go, and it is important that we actually use them.

However, we should not get stuck focusing on the raft itself, examining it, intellectualizing about it, and failing to actually use it to cross the river. Likewise, the teachings should not be revered or deified in and of themselves.

In Sanskrit, the teachings are described as a skillful method, or upaya. Another analogy describes the path as a finger, pointing at the moon. The finger is not the moon; the path is not the destination.

In a sense, the long journey on the path to awakening begins with the first vague sense of impermanence, the first feeling that the true nature of the universe is flow —constantly becoming, rather than a state of being.

Once a person begins to see that unskillful actions sooner or later bring about negative results, and that skillful, good actions ultimately bring about positive results, the momentum naturally leads to a skillful, ethical Buddhist life.

This momentum creates confidence in the rightness of the teachings, as predicted in the Kalama Sutta, and pushes the student further along the path.

The follower becomes a "Buddhist" when they

express an inner resolve to "take refuge" in the three jewels: the Buddha, the Dharma, and the Sangha.

The components of the path are described in terms that all include the word "Samma". The word Samma in Sanskrit is often translated as "right".

However, this word can have connotations in English that are not quite correct, considering the original context. Specifically, it means something closer to complete, true, perfected, proper, thorough, or whole.

The steps of the Eightfold Path are as follows:

1. Point of view (*Samma-Ditthi*).

2. Intention (Samma-*Sankappa*).

3. Speech (*Samma-Vaca*).

4. Action (*Samma-Kammanta).*

5. Livelihood (*Samma-Ajiva*).

6. Energy (*Samma-Vayama*).

7. Awareness (*Samma-Sati*).

8. Concentration (*Samma-Samadhi*).

Developing a complete point of view means honing our ability to see the truth of impermanence in reality. Perfecting our intention can be thought of as mentally preparing to pursue the path, compassion and enlightenment with one's whole being.

When your point of view and one's intention are 'right', it is important to ensure that your speech reflects the Dharma as well. This way of communicating will be gentle, truthful and full of compassion.

The aspect of the Eightfold Path that concerns one's actions focuses on the subtle and complex ethics of Buddhist practice. One works to ensure that one's behavior in the world reflects truth and compassion as well, in all ways.

The choice of your livelihood is fundamental to a life of commitment to the truth, because your mind naturally creates thoughts associated with the goal of one's livelihood.

If you are an artist, for example, you are likely to create beauty, and think healthy thoughts, not opposed to Buddhist teachings.

If, on the other hand, you are working in a slaughterhouse, you are spending hours every day thinking about, and participating in, the killing of other sentient beings. These thoughts and actions work against the upward, positive direction of the path to enlightenment.

Right, or complete, energy refers to consciously focusing our power on positive transformation for ourselves and for other beings.

We work to become aware of not only ourselves, our thoughts, feelings and our non-self, but the true nature of reality as it permeates everything and everyone around us. In other words, we work towards complete awareness.

The last "step" in the Eightfold Path – Samma Samadhi – means concentration of mind on a single object. It can also be taken to mean absorption in the most complete form of meditation. When this deep, all-encompassing meditation and concentration extends to a person's whole being, he or she is said to be fully enlightened, and to have achieved Buddahood.

As you move along the Eightfold Path, every aspect of your life choices and behaviors becomes involved in the practice — the way you interpret what happens, the way you feel, think and communicate, and your choice of livelihood.

Chapter 9: Meditation

"Meditation brings wisdom; lack of mediation leaves ignorance.

Know what leads you forward and what holds you back, and choose the path that leads to wisdom."

- Buddha

Meditation is fundamental to the practice of Buddhism, following the Eightfold Path and increasing one's understanding of the Four Noble Truths.

Right effort, or complete effort, involves directing our mind and energy towards developing right awareness (right mindfulness). Right effort succeeds in producing the right perception of the truths of existence, including ourselves, accomplishments, materials things, and the people around us.

Clearly, if our bodies are saturated with sensory input, and our minds are caught up in poisonous thoughts — about the future, past, daily concerns and so forth – we will likely be unable to see the true nature of reality.

Meditation involves calming the body and the mind — opening the possibility of seeing the impermanence of all we desire. Focusing the mind on simple, immediate activities such as the breath, keeps your mind focused in the present.

When you are focused on the present, on a simple truth or a simple process, you implicitly understand, as a byproduct, that you are not actually living in the future or the past.

You understand that the suffering caused by focusing on time, other than the now, is something you can free yourself from.

Mindfulness meditation is thus the conscious guiding of your mind – as opposed to allowing your mind to remain on autopilot, fixated on unhealthy attachments and mired in suffering. The practice of meditation has great benefits for both your mental state and your body.

Recent scientific studies have confirmed some of the psychological and physical benefits of meditating. Depression, stress, and other conditions such as binge eating, showed marked improvement in those who meditated regularly.

Practitioners have even had clear physical changes in their brain. These changes are called neuroplasticity. This neuroplasticity has been observed in areas of the brain associated with attention, emotional regulation and greater resilience to negative or stressful events.

For those who suffer mood swings and depressive episodes, practicing meditation can enable them to guide their minds away from the negative feelings.

Breaking this focus on negative thoughts, self-criticism, and worries allows room for greater perspective on the needlessness of such thoughts. Additionally, it allows your body to experience periods of relief from the physical effects of depression.

Immune benefits (such as antibody production), increased number of enzymes that contribute to cell longevity, and better regulation of mind-body signals around hunger and self-image can also be gained by practicing mindfulness meditation.

As awareness of the many boons of meditation becomes more widespread, mindfulness and other practices are being incorporated into schools, hospitals and workplaces. This means that meditation can be pursued as part of a Buddhist community, as an independent practice, as part of a course, or as a clinical intervention.

There is no single formula for cultivating mindfulness, and meditation techniques can be adapted to your individual needs and goals. Getting into the practice is simple and completely free — all you need is your mind and a quiet space.

If you are interested, you do not need to seek out a guru or trainer. You can get a quick start on your own by following a number of simple steps. Let us go through them now.

Classic Mindfulness Meditation — Step-by-Step

Before you begin: Choose a location where your body will be comfortable. You may want to use a pillow to sit on. Ideally, this location will be quiet and peaceful.

Be sure to minimize noise distractions where possible. Set up an hourglass or timer in front of you — 15 or 20 minutes of meditation is a great way to begin your practice.

1. Settle into a meditation posture, in which you will remain for the duration you have decided on. Sit in such a way that you can relax, and at the same time develop alertness. Keeping a more or less straight back is recommended.

2. Inhale and exhale through your nose.

3. Observe your breath, but do not try to control it.

4. Slowly do a mental scan of your whole body. Start with your toes and think about each one, observe them and let go of any tension that may be held there.

   Continue to move your focus up throughout your body until you reach the top of your head, consciously releasing tension in each part.

5. As you breathe normally, simply observe your body taking the breath in and letting the breath go.

As you focus on your breath, you will likely find that other thoughts appear in your mind.

A vital part of your mindfulness practice is learning to observe these thoughts, without judgment, and letting them go, guiding your consciousness to return to focus on your breath.

If your mind wanders, come back to experiencing the physical sensations of the breath, and begin counting again.

6. As you breathe out, pay attention to the sense of letting go, the relaxation of the body and the calming of your mind. Imagine yourself letting go of thoughts, judgments, attachments and anything else that might impede your immersion in the truth.

7. The final step. Start counting your outgoing breaths until you reach the number 10. Then, start over and continue this cycle (1-10, 1-10, etc.) Do this for at least five minutes.

Bring as much patience into the process as possible. It is normal for a lot of thoughts to arise, and from time to time you will completely forget you are supposed to be following your breath. Distraction is a normal part of the beginner's meditation experience.

You can build your practice by first doing in-, then out-, then continuous breathing. When your daily meditation is focused on the in-breaths, imagine that you are breathing in clarity, compassion, peacefulness, awakening.

Your practice should evolve to focus on the subtle sensations of the breath going in and out, and the effects on the body.

Mantras

As your ability develops, you may occasionally want to use other focus points for your meditation. Many practitioners focus on mantras, or specific words, as they meditate.

The following are some Sanskrit mantras that have

been used by serious practitioners since the beginning:

• Om
Translation: The sound of the universe.
Chanting Om creates harmonic resonance with the universe. When we chant Om, it creates vibrations at 432 hertz, which is said to be the natural musical pitch of the universe.

• Om Mani Padme Hum
Translation: Om is the sound of the universe. Ma establishes ethics. Ni establishes patience. Pad establishes perseverance. Me establishes concentration. Hum establishes wisdom.

• Lokah Samastah Sukhino Bhavantu
Translation: May all beings everywhere be happy and free, and may the thoughts, words, and actions of my own life contribute in some way to that happiness and to freedom for all.

Here are some English phrases popularly used as mantras:

- "Where I am right now, is exactly where I need to be."
- "I have a purpose in this life."
- "I surround myself by those who make me better."
- "I am a magnet for joy, love, and abundance."
- "I am enough."
- "Every day in every way, I'm getting better and better."
- "I change my thoughts, I change my world."
- "I am at peace with what is, what was, and what will be.

Other foci for meditation include mandalas, flowers, candles or other simple objects you can use as starting points for clear, pure intent.

This will allow your mind and body to relax, and you will gain perspective on the flow of thoughts and feelings that shape your life.

If you are interested in practicing mindful meditation in your everyday life, but cannot place yourself in an appropriate meditation posture and setting, there are still ways for you to practice.

Mindfulness can be practiced throughout the day in many different circumstances. When you are sitting on the bus, or standing somewhere waiting for a friend or family member, you can consciously guide your attention to the now. You can appreciate the present, be still, and be grateful for this moment.

Being in nature is often conducive to developing mindfulness. Observing the landscape, smelling the scents of flowers, listening to birds chirping etc.

Music is also very useful. You can focus on the sounds, melodies, and voices, as well as your emotional reactions.

Chapter 10:
Buddhism In Everyday Life

"What we are today comes from our thoughts of yesterday, and our present thoughts build our life of tomorrow.

Our life is the creation of our mind."

- Buddha

Buddhists talk about followers as those who regard the Dharma as a refuge. By this, they mean people who see Buddhism as a means of finding peace based on the truth of existence.

Followers of the Buddha are committed to practicing the teachings and incorporating Buddhist principles — of loving-kindness, mindfulness and compassion — into all that they do.

They must evaluate their actions in the light of Buddhist truths — in the light of their beliefs in emptiness, kindness and compassion.

As Buddhists, we should work to become increasingly aware of how our thoughts shape our entire experience of reality. As we discuss and apply the teachings, we begin to develop a deeper understanding of Buddhist wisdom and compassion.

Sincere engagement with Buddhist practices offers a means of gaining perspective on life and all that you experience in it; a way that offers greater feelings of peace and calm, relief from suffering, and even improved physical health.

Practical Application Of Buddhism

Practicing Buddhism in your everyday life involves a slight shift in your daily routines, and in the way in which you interpret what happens to you.

An activity you may want to add to your routine is a short morning meditation — 15-20 minutes after you wake up. This will let you to start the day with a clear mind and a greater sense of peace.

During your normal day – your self-care, commute, meals, day at work, your relationships with others – there are many opportunities to practice Buddhism.

As you go through these day-to-day activities, you will want to observe the three marks of existence around you: the impermanence of things, how clinging to them leads to unsatisfactoriness, and the ways in which your thoughts, feelings and attributes are not equal to "you" (the Not-Self, and the five skandhas).

One way of reinforcing this perspective on your life is to reflect on your thoughts – even just for a few moments – as you participate in your day-to-day activities. You can bring your mind to be wholly present in the moment. Focus on your breath, the smells around you, and the experience of this particular moment in time.

Spreading Peace & Loving-Kindness

"We will develop and cultivate the liberation of mind by loving kindness, make it our vehicle, make it our basis, stabilize it, exercise ourselves in it, and fully perfect it."

- Buddha

Once a person has found peace in their own heart, they can begin to bring peace and relief to others as well. Peace and loving kindness brings a joy that cannot be found in, much less created by, material objects.

As you observe people, clothing, cars, and other objects during your day, take the opportunity to consciously remind yourself that attachment to material things does not bring you lasting peace. If you can, see impermanence at work in the world, and accept everything as it is.

In order to practice loving kindness, you must always be ready to let go of selfishness, and show the right path to others. Combatting selfishness in others must be done through example and through discourse, since the source of unskillful actions is in the mind.

It is much more effective to fight negative influences with the mind, and with one's example of non-violence, than to do so with retaliation. Indeed, the very nature of the thought process of retaliation increases anger and hatred.

True charity is to give something without any thought to consequence or reward. A charitable act does not make the other person feel indebted, nor is charity ever used to create implicit control over another person.

While most people are grateful for kindness, many forget to express this in a way that the giver understands. The truest form of charity, however, does not require any kind of thanks – the giver is satisfied to know he or she has acted with a generous intention.

Practicing loving-kindness, charity and compassion towards all beings is an important part of living a Buddhist life. In your acknowledgement that existence is suffering, you will become more compassionate toward all other living creatures, recognizing that they, too, are going through hard times.

Showing compassion to all — human beings and animals, as well as the environment at large — relieves suffering, and can provide a glimpse of the Dharma for others. As such, it is part of Buddhist practice to live in a way that embodies compassion. Each being can spread kindness, peace and contentment in life.

During the day, you may want to pause to observe your thoughts about the people you encounter. There may be opportunities to simply say to yourself, "I have compassion for that old man I see struggling to walk" or "that woman was very rude to me — she's probably having a terrible day".

If you can show other people compassion through your acceptance, your kindness, your actions, that is even better. The skillful thoughts, habits, and actions of compassion and loving-kindness will become easier and more instinctual the more you practice them.

At the end of the day, you may want to review the waking hours in your mind, and make a point of noticing impermanence, attachments and suffering. In this way, you can practice having perspective on both the good and the bad things that occur in your life.

The events and situations that you perceive as being "bad" show you the ways in which you are still attached to things that are impermanent, to aspects of yourself that you are clinging to. As we have discussed, it is the clinging to impermanent things – which inevitably change – that causes the suffering.

Serious Hardship & Adversity

"The secret of health for both mind and body is not to mourn for the past, not to worry about the future, or not to anticipate troubles, but to live in the present moment wisely and earnestly."

- Buddha

As we go through life, we will inevitably experience adversity and serious hardship at different points in our journey. These periods of intense challenge and pain can take many forms.

Facing death, serious illness, and the loss of a loved one are some of the most challenging moments for any human being to endure.

The way we confront these challenges, and the way we think about what is happening to us, plays a very important role in our spiritual development and overall well-being.

A Buddhist monk named William Tran described his

experience in confronting cancer diagnosis and treatment. He conveyed an interesting blend of appreciation for both modern medicine and its physical effects, as well as Buddhist practice and teachings for the mind and spirit.

He reminds us that accepting the truth and living in the present moment are essential. This does not, however, mean giving up. It means accepting the nature of the challenge to one's health, planning for the future, yet living consciously for the now.

Tran recommends that people trust in their medical teams, and not to focus on stress and uncertainty. Instead, he suggests that people should keep up their meditation practice, and shift their focus towards things that are still within their influence.

In a 2015 interview with the Huffington Post, Tran shared some advice for others going through cancer:

"Face reality. Deal with your stress right now. Doctors can take care of the body, but they cannot take care of the mind.

Accept what you have right now. Face it directly and deal with it. If you accept the facts and ask for help, your mind will calm down. The medicine will kick in."

William Tran's cancer treatment was eventually successful, and he returned home to his temple with even more confidence in the Buddhist teachings.

His personal comments are echoed far and wide in both modern and historical Buddhist literature. As you now know, adhering to the truths of existence and accepting impermanence are foundations of a Buddhist perspective on all that causes suffering.

Buddhists believe that after death, a soul will be reborn, according to the karmic energy it has created in this lifetime. As long as the soul is attached to this life, and to the extent it has not succeeded in attaining Nirvana, it must experience rebirth in the cycle of samsara.

Only those who have detached themselves from all craving for unattainable permanence will be released from the cycle of death and rebirth. Only these souls will attain their final goal: Nirvana.

When death occurs, Buddhists appreciate the impermanence and Not-Self in the person who has died, and that the cycle of samsara will continue.

They also participate, with compassion and loving-kindness, in the rituals and mourning that accompany the death.

Perspective On Life, Milestones & Relationships

"To support mother and father, to cherish partner and children, and to be engaged in peaceful occupation – this is the greatest blessing."

- Buddha

Most modern societies celebrate the importance of major life events, such as marriage, having children, and attaining professional milestones. The ways in which modern society interprets these events and achievements can contribute to our attachments and delusions, because they are often presented as indications of a person's worth, the meaning in their lives, or as a permanent "good" that has been achieved.

In the light of the Buddha's teachings about the nature of existence (the three marks, the Four Noble Truths, the five skandhas, and the Eightfold Path), we recognize that these changes are ephemeral. There is falseness in the way society leads us to think of and care about these happenings.

At the same time, these important events in a human life are not necessarily seen to be meaningless in the context of Buddhism, in spite of its emphasis on the truth of impermanence.

Those who renounce a worldly life, such as Buddhist monks and other ascetics, keep away from social institutions like marriage to avoid entanglements and complications.

Without secular commitments, monks can remain

dedicated to their spiritual practice, and to serving and teaching others.

However, the Buddha did not insist that followers must abandon worldly lives and relationships. He delivered many discourses on the life of lay followers.

In a discourse known as the Sigalovada Sutta, the Buddha explained his perspective on proper social relationships within the family and the community. The foundation for all these essential relationships is the mutual acceptance of responsibilities between people.

The story of the Sigala is relayed as follows:
One morning, the Buddha saw a man, Sigala, bowing in six directions immediately after his bath. This was his morning ritual that he honored every day in memory of his own father.

His father had believed that one must honor the gods that lived in each direction: above, below, east, west, north and south.

He had believed that if one honored the gods in this

way, they would be pleased, and would reward the faithful with prosperity and good fortune.

When he saw Sigala bowing to the six directions, the Buddha explained his perspective on this ritual. His interpretation was that parents are represented by the east, teachers are represented by the south, wife or husband is represented by the west, friends are represented by the north, religious teachers are represented by above, and employees are represented by below.

In other words, honoring the six directions is, and should be, honoring the important people in one's life and development. These relationships are fundamental — honoring them is valuable, and will lead to greater happiness in life.

According to Buddhist teachings, it is important to honor these relationships by respectfully fulfilling one's responsibilities to the others: parents, children, friends, spouses, teachers, and employees.

As with bowing to the six directions, fulfilling one's social relationship responsibilities leads to experiencing good fortune, and to a stronger social fabric as a whole.

Buddhist spiritual leaders describe social relationships, friendships, and especially marriage in very similar terms. They explain that every relationship is a commitment to others in a community; everyone involved should be able to count on each other, responsibly upholding their parts of the relationship.

The Buddhist conception of marriage serves as a contrast to some modern notions of romantic love, and finding one's soulmate. According Buddhist thinking, a good, worthwhile marriage results from friendship, loyalty and mutual support.

The institution of marriage and family provides a strong basis for the development of culture. In spite of their focus on impermanence and contemplative practice, Buddhists recognize the role marriage and other social relationships can and should play in providing safety and support for individuals. A marriage should be a safe, supportive and comfortable partnership.

In marriage, each partner takes on responsibilities and activities according to the partners' respective skills, through mutual agreement.

Neither partner is considered superior — the union of two people works best when loving kindness, compassion and commitment to Buddhist ideals are at the core of the partnership.

Thus, it is clear that Buddhism can be practiced by any person, regardless of his or her attachments to family and community. You do not need to be an ascetic monk to practice meditation, loving-kindness and gentleness towards all.

As Buddha recommended in the Kalama Sutta, people can, and should, feel free to explore the teachings of Buddhism for themselves, and observe the effects of relief from suffering in their lives.

The truth of the Dharma will become manifest in the experience of observing and accepting impermanence, as well as practicing mindfulness and compassion.

Conclusion

The strength of the Buddhist tradition and its many variations over two and a half thousand years is a testament to the value that human beings find in its insights and practices.

Countless heavy volumes have been published on every single topic we have touched on in this beginner's guide. If this book piqued your interest, you are encouraged to seek out additional, more exhaustive resources, including translations of the original texts. These will explain various aspects of Buddhist thought in extensive detail, and from multiple angles.

If you are strongly drawn to the Buddhist lifestyle, there are plenty of temples and smaller communities all over the world that you can join.

However, if that is not for you, keep in mind that Buddhist practice can be undertaken by any individual at any time — there is no need for a priest or other intermediaries.

The path is always there for those who are ready to walk it.

Printed in Poland
by Amazon Fulfillment
Poland Sp. z o.o., Wrocław